The Train

A Division of The McGraw·Hill Companies

Columbus, Ohio

www.sra4kids.com

SRA/McGraw-Hill

A Division of The **McGraw·Hill** *Companies*

Send all inquiries to:
SRA/McGraw-Hill
8787 Orion Place
Columbus, OH 43240-4027

ISBN 0-07-569755-6
   3 4 5 6 7 8 9 DBH 05 04 03 02

When I was five, a train ran past this field.
The main track was up on the hill.

Under the daisies, you can see the remains of the track.
The rails are made of steel. The rails now make a trail.

The train had plainly painted cars.
The cars were filled with grain.
The train went from the farms to a
quaint, little city.
The horn wailed. It never failed.

The train had sacks of mail.
It gained speed from the quaint, little city
to the big city.
It made the trip daily, rain or shine.

I would wait and wave at the train.
The engineer on the train would wave
back.

The train stopped running
when I was six.
I still miss hearing the faint
rumble of the train.